W9-CDD-188

Cool Mexican Cooking

Fun and Tasty Recipes for Kids

Lisa Wagner

TO ADULT HELPERS

You're invited to assist up-and-coming chefs! As children learn to cook, they develop new skills, gain confidence, and make some delicious food. What's more, it's a lot of fun!

Efforts have been made to keep the recipes in this book authentic yet simple. You will notice that some of the recipes are more difficult than others. Be there to help children with these recipes, but encourage them to do as much as they can on their own. Also encourage them to try new foods and experiment with their own ideas. Building creativity into the cooking process encourages children to think like real chefs.

Before getting started, set some ground rules about using the kitchen, cooking tools, and ingredients. Most importantly, adult supervision is a must whenever a child uses the stove, oven, or sharp tools.

So, put on your aprons and stand by. Let your young chefs take the lead. Watch and learn. Taste their creations. Praise their efforts. Enjoy the culinary adventure!

visit us at www.abdopublishing.com

Published by ABDO Publishing Company, a division of ABDO, P.O. Box 398166, Minneapolis, Minnesota 55439. Copyright © 2011 by Abdo Consulting Group, Inc. International copyrights reserved in all countries. No part of this book may be reproduced in any form without written permission from the publisher. Checkerboard Library™ is a trademark and logo of ABDO Publishing Company.

Printed in the United States of America, North Mankato, Minnesota
102010
032013

♺ PRINTED ON RECYCLED PAPER

Design and Production: Colleen Dolphin, Mighty Media, Inc.
Art Direction: Colleen Dolphin
Series Editor: Liz Salzmann
Food Production: Frankie Tuminelly
Photo Credits: Colleen Dolphin, iStockphoto/Sandra O'Claire, Photodisc, Shutterstock

The following manufacturers/names appearing in this book are trademarks: Kemps®, Market Pantry®, Morton's® Old El Paso®, Pyrex®

Library of Congress Cataloging-in-Publication Data

Wagner, Lisa, 1958-
  Cool Mexican cooking : fun and tasty recipes for kids / Lisa Wagner.
     p. cm. -- (Cool world cooking)
  Includes index.
  ISBN 978-1-61714-662-6
  1. Cooking, Mexican--Juvenile literature. I. Title.
  TX716.M4W32 2011
  641.5972--dc22
                              2010022194

Table of Contents

EXPLORE THE FOODS OF MEXICO! 4

THE BASICS 6

THE TOOL BOX 8

COOL COOKING TERMS 10

THE COOLEST INGREDIENTS 12

MEXICAN EXTRAS 16

TASTY TOSTADAS 18

SAVORY MIXED SALAD 20

AMAZING MEXICAN RICE 22

TEMPTING TAQUITOS 24

TERRIFIC TORTILLA SOUP 26

GREEN ENCHILADA CASSEROLE 28

WRAP IT UP! 30

GLOSSARY 31

WEB SITES 31

INDEX 32

Explore the Foods of Mexico!

Are you ready to make some great Mexican food? Mexicans have been eating corn, beans, chiles, tomatoes, avocados, fruit, and fish for hundreds of years. Foods such as corn, chiles, and tomatoes grow well in Mexico. This is because of the long, hot growing season there. Avocados grow best on mountainsides. So if you think Mexico has mountains, you are correct!

When Spanish explorers came to Mexico in the 1500s, they brought new foods. These foods included rice, garlic, onion, spices, herbs, beef, **pork**, and **poultry**. The recipes in this book include some of these Spanish influences.

Spicy food is popular in hot climates because it makes people sweat. When a person sweats, he or she feels cooler. You will find chiles and chili powder used in this book. But don't worry! These recipes offer a little kick, not unpleasant hotness. Are you ready for a tasty Mexican adventure? Put on your aprons and off we go!

GET THE PICTURE!

When a step number in a recipe has a dotted circle around it, look for the picture that goes with it. The circle around the photo will be the same color as the step number.

4 →

HOW DO YOU SAY THAT?

You may come across some Spanish words you've never heard of in this book. Don't worry! There's a pronunciation guide on page 30!

The Basics

Get going in the right direction
with a few important basics!

ASK PERMISSION

Before you cook, get permission to use the kitchen, cooking tools, and ingredients. When you need help, ask. Always get help when you use the stove or oven.

GET ORGANIZED

- Being well organized is a chef's secret ingredient for success!

- Read through the entire recipe before you do anything else.

- Gather all your cooking tools and ingredients.

- Get the ingredients ready. The list of ingredients tells how to prepare each item.

- Put each prepared ingredient into a separate bowl.

- Read the recipe instructions carefully. Do the steps in the order they are listed.

GOOD COOKING TAKES PREP WORK

Many ingredients need preparation before they are used. Look at a recipe's ingredients list. Some ingredients will have words such as chopped, sliced, or grated next to them. These words tell you how to prepare the ingredients.

Give yourself plenty of time and be patient. Always wash fruits and vegetables. Rinse them well and pat them dry with a **towel**. Then they won't slip when you cut them. After you prepare each ingredient, put it in a separate prep bowl. Now you're ready!

BE SMART, BE SAFE

- If you use the stove or oven, you need an adult with you.

- Never use the stove or oven if you are home alone.

- Always get an adult to help with the hot jobs, such as frying with oil.

- Have an adult nearby when you are using sharp tools such as knives, peelers, graters, or food processors.

- Always turn pot handles to the back of the stove. This helps prevent accidents and spills.

- Work slowly and carefully. If you get hurt, let an adult know right away!

BE NEAT, BE CLEAN

- Start with clean hands, clean tools, and a clean work surface.

- Tie back long hair so it stays out of the way and out of the food.

- Roll up your sleeves.

- An apron will protect your clothes from spills and splashes.

- Chef hats are **optional**!

KEY SYMBOLS

In this book, you will see some symbols beside the recipes. Here is what they mean.

HOT STUFF!
The recipe requires the use of a stove or oven. You need adult assistance and supervision.

SUPER SHARP!
A sharp tool such as a peeler, knife, or grater is needed. Get an adult to stand by.

NUT ALERT!
Some people can get very sick if they eat nuts. If you are cooking with nuts, let people know!

EVEN COOLER!
This symbol means adventure! Give it a try! Get inspired and invent your own cool ideas.

No Germs Allowed!

Raw eggs and raw meat have bacteria in them. These bacteria are killed when food is cooked. But they can survive out in the open and make you sick! After you handle raw eggs or meat, wash your hands, tools, and work surfaces with soap and water. Keep everything clean!

The Tool Box

A box on the bottom of the first page of each recipe lists the tools you need.
When you come across a tool you don't know, turn back to these pages.

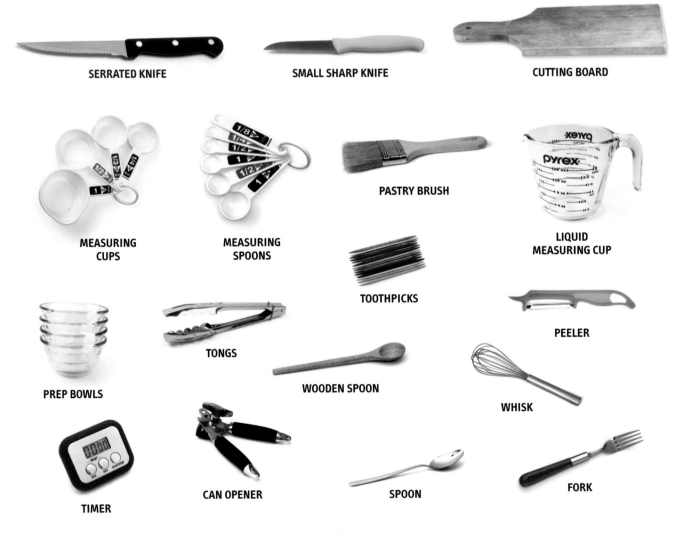

SERRATED KNIFE

SMALL SHARP KNIFE

CUTTING BOARD

MEASURING CUPS

MEASURING SPOONS

PASTRY BRUSH

LIQUID MEASURING CUP

TOOTHPICKS

PEELER

PREP BOWLS

TONGS

WOODEN SPOON

WHISK

TIMER

CAN OPENER

SPOON

FORK

JUICER

BAKING SHEET

SERVING PLATE

BLENDER

FRYING PAN

SAUCEPAN

POT HOLDERS

SOUP POT

GRATER

PAPER TOWELS

KITCHEN TOWELS

MIXING BOWLS

9 × 9-INCH BAKING PAN

Cool Cooking Terms

Here are some basic cooking terms and the actions that go with them. Whenever you need a reminder, just turn back to these pages.

FIRST THINGS FIRST

Always wash fruit and vegetables well. Rinse them under cold water. Pat them dry with a **towel**. Then they won't slip when you cut them.

CHOP

Chop means to cut things into small pieces with a knife.

GRATE

Grate means to shred something into small pieces using a grater.

JUICE

To *juice* a fruit means to remove the juice from its insides by squeezing it or using a juicer.

MIX

Mix means to stir ingredients together, usually with a large spoon.

MASH

Mash means to press down and smash food with a fork or potato masher.

SLICE

Slice means to cut food into pieces of the same thickness.

MINCE

Mince means to cut the food into the tiniest possible pieces. Garlic is often minced.

SAUTÉ

Sauté means to fry quickly in a pan using a small amount of oil or butter.

PEEL

Peel means to remove the skin, often with a peeler.

WHISK

Whisk means to beat quickly by hand with a whisk or fork.

The Coolest Ingredients

TOMATO

CELERY

ICEBERG LETTUCE

RADISHES

WHITE ONION

TOMATILLOS

LIMES

BLACK BEANS

AVOCADOS

CARROTS

GREEN BELL PEPPER

GROUND CUMIN

CHILI POWDER

GROUND CINNAMON

DRIED OREGANO

DRIED THYME

BAY LEAVES

JALAPEÑO PEPPERS

GARLIC CLOVES

SALT

CILANTRO

SCALLIONS

13

CHEDDAR CHEESE

MONTEREY JACK CHEESE

COLBY-JACK CHEESE

CHICKEN BROTH

DICED TOMATOES

CANNED TOMATO PURÉE

VANILLA ICE CREAM

TOSTADA SHELLS

CORN TORTILLAS

TORTILLA CHIPS

DICED GREEN CHILES

SOUR CREAM

SALSA

HEAVY CREAM

VEGETABLE OIL

OLIVE OIL

CANOLA OIL

SEMISWEET CHOCOLATE CHIPS

VANILLA EXTRACT

LONG-GRAIN WHITE RICE

GROUND BEEF

CHICKEN BREASTS

Allergy Alert!

Some people have a reaction when they eat certain foods. If you have any allergies, you know what it's all about. An allergic reaction can require emergency medical help. Nut allergies can be especially **dangerous**. Before you serve anything made with nuts or peanut oil, ask if anyone has a nut allergy.

Now That's Hot!

Jalapeño peppers are very hot. Always wear rubber gloves when you chop jalapeño peppers. Then wash your hands, the cutting board, and the knife with soap and water right away. Be careful never to touch a cut pepper and then touch your eyes or nose. Ouch!

Mexican Extras

Take your Mexican cooking to the next level! The ideas on these pages will show you how.

SUPER SHREDDED CHICKEN

Makes about 3 cups

INGREDIENTS

1 pound boneless, skinless chicken breasts
1 bay leaf
1 teaspoon dried oregano
½ teaspoon dried thyme
15-ounce can chicken broth

Tip:
You can make more shredded chicken or ground beef than you need and freeze the leftovers! Remember too that beans are always a great meat substitute.

1 Put all the ingredients in a medium saucepan.

2 Bring to a boil over medium-high heat. Reduce the heat to medium and cook for 20 minutes.

3 Cover the saucepan. Turn off the heat and let the pan sit until cool.

4 Remove the chicken and rinse it with cold water.

5 Use a fork to shred the chicken.

GREAT GROUND BEEF

Makes about 2 cups

INGREDIENTS

1 pound ground beef
1 cup chopped white onion
1 clove garlic, minced
8-ounce can tomato purée
⅓ cup water
½ teaspoon salt
1 tablespoon chili powder
½ teaspoon dried oregano
½ teaspoon ground cumin

1 Put the meat, onion, and garlic in a frying pan. Cook over medium heat. As the meat browns, break it up with a wooden spoon. Cook until the meat is no longer pink.

2 Have an adult help you drain and **discard** the grease from the pan.

3 Stir in the tomato purée, water, salt, and spices. Cook over medium heat for 5 to 10 minutes, stirring occasionally.

GOT-TO-HAVE-IT GUACAMOLE

Makes about 2 cups

INGREDIENTS

2 very ripe medium avocados
1 small tomato, chopped
½ cup minced white onion
1 tablespoon fresh lime juice
¼ teaspoon salt

1 Cut the avocados in half and remove the pits.

2 Scoop the avocado from the skin and put it in a bowl.

3 Mash the avocado with a fork until it is mostly smooth.

4 Add the other ingredients and stir with the fork until blended.

MAJORLY DELICIOUS HOT FUDGE SAUCE

Makes about 1½ cups

INGREDIENTS

½ cup heavy cream
⅓ cup water
12 ounces semisweet chocolate chips
1 teaspoon ground cinnamon
½ teaspoon vanilla extract
vanilla ice cream

1 Bring cream and water to a boil in a small saucepan over medium-high heat. Remove pan from heat.

2 Add chocolate and cinnamon. Stir until chocolate is melted and sauce is smooth.

3 Mix in vanilla extract until well blended.

4 Serve over vanilla ice cream.

Tasty Tostadas

Toasted tortillas topped with your favorite ingredients!

MAKES 12 TOSTADAS

INGREDIENTS

- ½ head iceberg lettuce, cut into ¼-inch strips
- 2 tomatoes, chopped
- 2 cups grated cheddar or colby-jack cheese
- 1 cup radishes, chopped
- 1 tablespoon olive oil
- 1 small white onion, minced
- 2 cups prepared shredded chicken or ground beef (page 16)
- 2 cloves garlic, minced
- ½ teaspoon dried oregano
- 2 tablespoons chili powder
- ½ teaspoon ground cumin
- ½ teaspoon salt
- ½ cup water
- 12 tostada shells

TOOLS: small sharp knife | measuring spoons | wooden spoon | timer
serrated knife | measuring cups | baking sheet | serving plate
cutting board | grater | tongs | spoons and forks
prep bowls | frying pan | pot holders

18

1 Preheat the oven to 350 degrees. Put the prepared lettuce, tomatoes, grated cheese, and radishes in small prep bowls. Set aside.

2 Heat the olive oil in a large frying pan. Add the onion and sauté over medium-high heat for 5 minutes.

3 Add the prepared chicken or beef and the garlic, oregano, chili powder, cumin, salt, and water. Cook over medium heat for 5 to 10 minutes, stirring occasionally.

4 Put the tostada shells on a baking sheet. Warm them in the oven for about 3 minutes. Remove from the oven and use tongs to gently put the tostadas on a serving plate.

5 Put 3 tablespoons of the chicken or beef on each tostada. Take the serving plate to the table. Set the prep bowls with the lettuce, tomatoes, grated cheese, and radishes on the table. Let everyone make their own tostadas just the way they like them!

Even Cooler!

You can add anything to your tostada! Try guacamole (page 17), sour cream, black beans, and rice!

Savory Mixed Salad

A simple dressing is this salad's best friend!

MAKES 6 SERVINGS

TOOLS: cutting board, small sharp knife, serrated knife, prep bowls, measuring spoons, juicer, peeler, grater, mixing bowls, whisk, two forks

20

1 Put the lettuce in the **salad** bowl. Tear it into bite-size pieces.

2 Add the bell pepper, scallions, radishes, carrots, and avocado.

 Put the lime juice, olive oil, garlic, salt, and chili powder in a small mixing bowl. Whisk until well blended. This is the dressing!

4 Pour the dressing over the vegetables and toss gently to mix.

5 Arrange the tomatoes over the top of the salad. Serve immediately.

Amazing Mexican Rice

This rice makes a great
side or main dish!

MAKES 8 SERVINGS

INGREDIENTS

1 cup long-grain white rice

2⅓ cups water

1 teaspoon salt

1 tablespoon olive oil

2 carrots, chopped

1 small white onion, minced

1 clove garlic, minced

1 stalk celery, chopped

14-ounce can **diced** tomatoes

1 teaspoon chili powder

TOOLS:

medium saucepan with cover	prep bowls	mixing bowl	wooden spoon
cutting board	measuring spoons	kitchen towel	timer
small sharp knife	measuring cups	fork	can opener

1 Put the rice, 2 cups water, and the salt in a medium saucepan. Bring to a boil over medium-high heat. Stir.

2 Cover the saucepan and turn the heat to low.

3 Let the rice cook over low heat for 18 minutes. Do not remove the cover.

4 Turn off the heat and let the rice sit for 10 minutes. Then take the cover off the pan.

5 Use a fork to separate the grains of rice. Put the rice in a mixing bowl and cover it with a kitchen **towel**.

6 Wash and dry the saucepan.

7 Heat the olive oil in the saucepan. Add the carrots, onion, garlic, and celery. Cook over medium heat for 10 minutes, stirring occasionally.

8 Add the **diced** tomatoes, chili powder, and ⅓ cup water. Cook for 5 minutes, stirring occasionally.

9 Add the rice to the saucepan and stir to blend well. Cook over low heat 1 to 2 minutes, stirring constantly. Serve.

Tempting Taquitos

This amazing snack is too tasty to miss!

MAKES 9 SERVINGS

INGREDIENTS

2 cups prepared ground beef (page 16)

8 ounces Monterey Jack cheese, grated

18 corn tortillas

canola oil

salt

guacamole (page 17)

salsa

TOOLS:
- frying pan
- tongs
- paper towels
- plate
- medium mixing bowl
- grater
- measuring spoons
- toothpicks
- baking sheet
- pastry brush
- pot holders
- timer

1 Preheat the oven to 450 degrees. Heat the frying pan over medium high heat. Lightly grease the frying pan. Just coat the surface with the oil so the tortilla won't stick.

2 Set a tortilla in the frying pan for 1 to 2 minutes, just until it is softened. Place it on a large plate and cover the plate with an upside-down mixing bowl. Repeat this step until all the tortillas are softened. Grease the frying pan from time to time as needed.

3 Take a tortilla and set it on your work surface. Put 2 tablespoons of ground beef and 1 tablespoon of cheese on the tortilla.

4 Roll the tortilla up and use a toothpick to hold it closed. Set it on a greased baking sheet. Repeat this step until all the tortillas are filled and rolled.

5 Brush each rolled tortilla (it is a taquito now) with canola oil and sprinkle with salt. Bake for 10 minutes. The outside should be **crispy** and the cheese should be melted.

6 Use tongs to set the hot taquitos on paper **towels** to drain any excess oil. Serve with guacamole and salsa for dipping. Taquitos are best eaten very warm right out of your hand.

Terrific Tortilla Soup

This zesty soup tastes great!

MAKES 6-8 SERVINGS

INGREDIENTS

2 limes, cut into wedges

1 cup sour cream

½ cup cilantro leaves

1 cup Monterey Jack cheese, grated

1 avocado, chopped

1 tablespoon olive oil

1 small white onion, chopped

3 cloves garlic, finely chopped

1 small can **diced** green chiles

4 cups chicken broth

28-ounce can diced tomatoes

½ teaspoon salt

½ teaspoon dried thyme

1 teaspoon dried oregano

1 teaspoon ground cumin

1 tablespoon chili powder

2 cups prepared shredded chicken (page 16)

1½ cups tortilla chips, broken into smaller pieces

TOOLS: cutting board · small sharp knife · prep bowls · measuring spoons · measuring cup · can opener · soup pot · wooden spoon · grater · timer

1. Put the prepared limes, sour cream, cilantro, grated cheese, and avocado in small prep bowls. Set aside.

2. Heat the oil in a soup pot or Dutch oven over medium-high heat. Add the onions and cook for 5 minutes, stirring occasionally.

 Add the garlic and chiles and cook for 2 minutes.

4. Add the broth, tomatoes, salt, thyme, oregano, cumin, and chili powder. Bring to a boil. Then reduce heat to low and simmer for 15 minutes.

5. Add the chicken and simmer for 5 minutes.

 To serve, put some broken tortilla chips in each bowl. Fill the bowls with soup.

7. Put the prepared ingredients from step 1 on the table. Let everyone **garnish** their own soup with the things they like best!

Tip

If you don't have time to make the shredded chicken, use roast chicken from a deli. Buy two ¾-inch slices. For this recipe, cut the slices into ¾-inch cubes.

Green Enchilada Casserole

INGREDIENTS

12 corn tortillas
vegetable oil for frying
12 tomatillos, papery husks removed
1 clove garlic, minced
½ teaspoon salt
6 stems of cilantro
3 cups shredded chicken (page 16)
2 cups grated Monterey Jack cheese
¾ cup sour cream
4 scallions, chopped

The first enchiladas were small fish wrapped in corn tortillas!

MAKES 8 SERVINGS

TOOLS: blender
saucepan
cutting board
small sharp knife
measuring spoons
measuring cups
grater
frying pan
plate
mixing bowls
wooden spoon
9 x 9-inch baking pan
timer
pot holders

1 Preheat the oven to 350 degrees. Heat 1 teaspoon vegetable oil in a frying pan over medium high heat. Cook the tortillas one at a time for about 1 minute on each side. Add small amounts of oil as needed to keep the tortillas from sticking to the pan. Set the tortillas on a plate. Cover them with a medium mixing bowl to keep them warm.

2 To make the green sauce, put the tomatillos, garlic, salt, and cilantro in a blender. Blend until smooth. Put the mixture in a saucepan. Bring to a boil over medium-high heat. Reduce heat to low. Simmer for 10 minutes, stirring occasionally.

3 In a large bowl, mix the chicken, 1 cup of the Monterey Jack cheese, sour cream, and 1 cup of the green sauce.

4 Grease the baking pan.

5 Put ⅓ cup of the chicken mixture on a tortilla and roll it up. Place it in the pan seam side down. Repeat this step until all the tortillas are filled.

6 Pour the remaining 1½ cups of green sauce over the tortillas. Sprinkle the remaining 1 cup of cheese and the scallions over the sauce.

7 Bake uncovered for 40 minutes.

Even Cooler!

For a spicier sauce, chop up half of a jalapeño pepper. Add it to the green sauce. See note on page 15 about working with jalapeño peppers.

Wrap it Up!

Now you know how to make **delicious** Mexican dishes! What did you learn? Did you try any new foods? Learning about recipes from around the world teaches you a lot. You learn about different **cultures**, climates, geography, and tastes.

Making international dishes also teaches you about new languages. Did you learn any new Spanish words in this book? These new words will help you sound like a native speaker. You'll be able to use them at restaurants and **grocery stores**.

Enchilada (en-chee-LAH-duh)

Guacamole (gwah-kuh-MOH-lay)

Taquito (tah-KEE-toh)

Tomatillo (toh-ma-TEE-oh)

Tortilla (tor-TEE-yuh)

Tostada (toh-STAH-duh)

Glossary

crispy – hard, thin, and easy to break.

culture – the behavior, beliefs, art, and other products of a particular group of people.

dangerous – able or likely to cause harm or injury.

delicious – very pleasing to taste or smell.

dice – cut into small cubes.

discard – to throw away.

garnish – to add small amounts of food to finish a dish.

grocery store – a place where you buy food items.

optional – something you can choose, but is not required.

pork – meat that comes from a pig.

poultry – birds, such as chickens or turkeys, raised for eggs or meat.

salad – a mixture of raw vegetables usually served with a dressing.

towel – a cloth or paper used for cleaning or drying.

Web Sites

To learn more about cool cooking, visit ABDO Publishing Company on the World Wide Web at **www.abdopublishing. com.** Web sites about cool cooking are featured on our Book Links page. These links are routinely monitored and updated to provide the most current information available.

Index

A

Adult help/permission, 6, 7
Allergies, 15

B

Bacteria, 7

C

Chicken, shredded, 16, 27
Chopping, 10
Cleanliness guidelines, 6, 7, 10
Cooking terms, 10–11

E

Enchilada casserole, 28–29

G

Grating, 10
Ground beef, 16
Guacamole, 17

H

Hot fudge sauce, 17

I

Ingredients
    cleanliness of, 6, 10
    common types of, 12–15
    preparation of, 6

J

Jalapeño peppers, 15, 29
Juicing, 10

L

Languages, learning about, 30

M

Mashing, 11
Mexico, food/cooking in, 4, 30
Mincing, 11
Mixed salad, 20–21
Mixing, 10

P

Peeling, 11
Permission, for cooking/kitchen use, 6, 7
Preparation, for cooking, 6

R

Recipes, reading of, 6
Rice, 22–23

S

Safety guidelines, 7, 15
Salad, 20–21
Sautéing, 11
Seasoning, 4, 15, 29
Shredded chicken, 16, 27
Slicing, 11
Stove/Oven use, 6, 7

T

Taquitos, 24–25
Tools
    cleanliness of, 7
    common types of, 8–9
    preparation of, 6
Tortilla soup, 26–27
Tortillas, recipes using, 18–19, 24–25, 26–27, 28–29
Tostadas, 18–19

W

Whisking, 11